I0422784

Name: shahnewaz Bhuiyan
street address:14700 Endsley Turn

city, state, Virginia zip: Woodbridge , 22193
phone:5712885112

Triassic moon

By:
Shahnewaz Bhuiyan

In the year 2029 not too distant future planet Eurora site : LV 223 and LV 228 a lost forbidden planet/moon called Eurora 30 kilometers from earth near distant solar system from planet mercury inhhabited with dinosaurs and dragons was settled by group of androids,aliens and mad scientists.It was a dangerous near suicide mission that they never think of. They use nanites/alien dragonflies to create perfect hybrid breed of alien dinosaurs and dragons.raptor rex,T-rex,Spinosaurus,,apatosaurus,ankylosaurus,,microceratus,avimimus,miasaur,fragillimus, ,prehistoric dragon,marine and mountain dragons, Utahraptor,etc. Long time ago when dinosaurs existed alien dragonflies known as psuodofiles sucked blood out of the dinos and get stuck in frozen icy chambers in antarctica.most of them although would fly off to outer space.Then alien psuodoflies gets collected by space nuclear alien physicists who collects artifacts and other fossils,they are called the bounty hunters.

The year is 2016 present day, group of space explorers find a crashed ship on the to the moon/planet called Eurora .they said its 30 kilometers from the planet earth he said.we are in terranova anymore we are in Eurora said the general .we are here for one thing and one thing only this organism they say in their homeland these creatures psuodofiles.I say its'a living hell. Who ever gets infacted by it they die.it releases nerotoxin and multiply by sucking any part of your body.these nasty looking can be tricky to pull of once it attaches to any you so, what do we do.anyone at all ,yes you in the back . we torch it . yes ,we torch it said he said with this hot 5000 magnesium burner . I know for lot of you young woman and men to catch up to the task of this expedition,some of you may die in this journey but, it's a sacrifice.I am willing to make. Gear up ladies, go go go go.awakens to find himself parachuting into an unfamiliar jungle. He meets several others who arrived in the same manner: Mexican drug cartel enforcer Cuchillo , Spetsnaz soldier Nikolai), Israel Defense Forces sniper Isabelle , Revolutionary United Front officer Mombasa, death row inmate,Yakuza enforcer Hanz, and a general practice doctor Edwin Stay close we are not alone in this moon or planet what ever this nightmare place is ,last time heard people got killed and never came back at all.is that true rico.yeah he was'nt so lucky.look over there. We have been spotted you see rico.rico: yeah it's too dark.well use the flare we some light in this situation.oh my god.ahhhhhhhhhhhhh help me.wilson you alright.wilson, someone talk to me damn it .i guess your on your on your own my friend i'll get contact and come back see if there is any survivors.good luck to you amigo.

What about me man what am I supposed to be doing.Rico : I don't know man find something useful like set up a camp fire while i get back.Rico: I'll get those damn radio's.where did you those

Radios last there in my bunker jeep,everything is fine. Soldier 1 : What's that all about. Private :bravo 1 do you copy over.bravo 10 do you copy over. I repeat we are under attack.Rico: can anyone hear me oh, god damn it gotta do everything by ourselves don't we.hello rico hello hello.yes general I read you over.rico here's what i want you to do.wait general i didn't catch last part .The phone is breaking up. booom.Rico!!! Rico!!

This is The story of Corporal Kraven ''Rico'' Rodriguez, former member of the Wolf Pack, a hispanic latino with some bad attitude was specialized military detachment whose members were trained in black ops by General Roland Bane. After a falling out with the group, rico was reassigned to a general military unit known as Whiskey Company. The team has been assembled to apprehend his former mentor and return him to Earth. After committing various war crimes, Bane had disappeared three years earlier only to surface on a backwater world. Unbeknownst to Whiskey Company, the planet is under the jurisdiction of the Mendel-Grumman (M-G) Corporation, and Bane is in command of a private army of M-G soldiers and equipment.

At first, the crew shuns rico, thinking that he is an inexperienced fighter, untrustworthy, and a liability. One particular member, Slade, has a personal grudge against Rico because his brother

Robert was also a member of Wolf Pack, and was killed in the same battle in Colombia from which Rico had reputedly fled, earning him his dubious reputation.

On approach to their destination, their starship is shot down from orbit and crash lands on the terraformed surface, where Rico quickly learns that the jungles covering the surface, even the planet are inhabited by alien hybrid dinosaurs and dragons. Despite being genetically engineered, the dinosaurs are wild and dangerous, and the M-G soldiers have been capturing them to be used as experimental weapons for General Bane, meaning a three-way battle between Whiskey Company, the M-G soldiers, and the dinosaurs takes place throughout the game. Upon crashing, many of Whiskey Company are killed by the crash or are either killed by dinosaurs or M-G soldiers.

are abruptly whisked away by billionaire richard raymond — founder and chief executive officer of International Genetic Technologies, or whisky— for a weekend visit to a "biological preserve" he has established on planet LV 223.

Upon arrival, the preserve is revealed to be triassic moon, a fertilization showcasing cloned dinosaurs. The animals have been recreated using damaged dinosaur DNA found in blood inside of gnats and alien ticks fossilized and preserved in cryogenic ice. Gaps in the genetic code have been filled in with reptilian, avian, or amphibian DNA. To control the population, all specimens on the moon are lysine-deficient females. raymond proudly touts whiskey's advances in genetic engineering and shows his guests through the planet's vast array of automated systems.

Mr.Eugene robert walters sr and molley journal october 21,2016 present time in eurora.I am australian-american and little bit of german.I used to be a zookeeper/documentarian.how did end up here you may ask.First of all I used to be a zoologist.taking care of animals in the zoo animals and so forth until that day it happened I was reassigned. Mr.Eugene you're being reassigned but, my work here isn't finished it is now said eurora main advocate .

Back at the Airforce base the main advocate speaks it is my privilage and honor to be hear today I am richard raymonds and welcome to our space exposition.it is my job to keep you alive and well.I want each and every one of you to gear up and be ready for any types of bad situation,all I want is your cooperation and support.thank you.Rico: command, this is command this is rico over.what the heck is going on out there.dinosaur and dragons everywhere lose.Rico, Rico all those animals on the east side of land with you.yeah

But, they are on a rampage killing our men.rico i want you look out if there anyone else who survived.Suddenly,a velociraptor-rex tries to attack rico but, starts the engine run the jeep.Rico: No,time to explain general .hang on. General: rico!Rico! Rico can you hear me get out of there.Rico.rico.damn it we lost rico but,the radio is still on.General: god have mercy,old jesus.

Command: Where are the others,I think they are on the west side of the fence.as rico aproches and run into eugene they are seen by a herd of triceratops.eugene says dont move any muscle.as he backs up a utahraptor sneeks up behind him.eugene says to rico run rico run as fast as you can.then they all ran together in a different direction and jumped of the waterfall.

Utahraptor stood watching from high ground until,it turned it's back and left.eugene says to rico you alright.rico says of i'm alright you tweet.

After that rico and eugene look out any others that made it out alive in the Eurora moon jungle.rico: hello can anyone hear me. Rico: oh yak.eugene and rico go on an abandoned cargo ship and finds no one but,bodies ripped to shreds.eugene:where is everyone.rico:all over the place.

So,rico i have one question are portuguese or something.rico says why.i'm sorry i was wondering.i'm el salvadorian and spanish.eugene: you're a latino colonial marine with some bad attitude.
What about me man what am I supposed to be doing.Rico : I don't know man find something useful like set up a camp fire while i get back.Rico: I'll get those damn radio's.where did you those

Eugene : is that a boat rico.I think so amigo.let get off this nightmare cargo ship.as they sail off they encounters giant crocodilians and t-rexs.as they sail they start shooting the t-rex on the head.eugene here's sniper rife and aim it on the head.shoot shoot.keep stooting eugene.

Here's a grenade throw it inside of the crocodile's mouth.eugene throws it and crocodile explodes into 50 pieces.

Then Eugene and rico encounters some nasty pteranodons.they slices and dices and eugene falls down in the pond of water where he gets followed by a megalodon as it grasp and swallow eugene.rico in shallow water and tells eugene to hang on.rico: eugene take my hand.eugene take his hand and get out of the pond as megalodon almost grabbed eugene but, failed.

Rico: stay hidden ,we must be getting close.eugene says i think this some type of cage.rico says for what rats.soon they discover prehistoric dragon attacks from above.rico:get away from me you rats with wings.then Eugene:thanks.rico:don't mansion it.Eugene:I really meant.rico:ever.as they left the swamp they encounter pack of ankylosaurus and stegosaurus.Eugene say oh,wow.rico says yeah whatever.
rico starts firing his shots.eugene says noooooo don't.it will make them agitated.then one of the dragon caught eugene drops him down to the dragon's nest. Rico: hold on i'm coming.as fires his last shots the dragons fly away from their nest.rico: looks like that one is out of the

way.Egune: luckily we didn't panic.rico: well,next time stay close your not good me dead.Eugene: your welcome.

Rico and Eugene gets chased by pack of raptors in the abandoned laboratory.as they ran they encounter herd of miasaurs.Euenge says head for the trees.then they climb up a tree to safety.other marines gets killed in the near jungle.eugene and rico are the only surviivors who make out safe.Next day eugenge and rico finds others who survived.at the big fence. Where are the others says rico .I need to find a gap here.They are followed by a spinosaurus rex.eugene says run.as the spino chased them down they found a hole they enter it and spino turns back.

Then rico and eugene climbs down a underground tunnel where they find spores of eggs where it's fertilized as farm.eugene: I think they are these dinosaur eggs as bait.rico what makes you think that.I think it was a secret project that was top secret.rico says sure it's big enough but look at the location.

As they walk past the eggs swarm of pseudo flies attack .M-G soldier recover and gets attacked by pseudo flies.wilson can you hear.rico we are under attack.M-G soldiers get fire hoses and burns up the pseudo flies.M-G soldier 1 : all clear.

rico hears a phone inside dinosaur droppings they dig it out and suddenly they encounter an allosaur.the allosaur smells and disappears.

M-G soldiers try to capture the spino with fish,unfortunately spino rampage on loose.then they shoot it down.nothing worked.so they nutralize it by sedate.
Then the spino falls real hard and sleeps.general bane says that's one down,two more to go.
After that they try to hunt down other dinosaurs while rico and eugene are spotted.eugene and rico waves their arms.rico:hey over here,eugene we are saved.out of nowhere an allosaur attacks the chopper. Rico and eugene runs into safety hidden from the allosaur.

The allosaur walks around sniffing for the next meal.eugene and rico under the broken jeep hiding from it. The allosaur finds no food as it leaves.

Rico and eugene sees a herd of plant eating dinosaurs.eugene say no sudden movements clearly they are not fake.rico: nobody will think these are fake.out of nowhere bunch of allosaur and utahraptors attack.eugene says they are blocking our way.rico: mother of god.. The rescue party is then caught in the middle of a pack of *utah raptor* hunting a herd of *brachiosaur* and Herb is killed along with four sailors. The rest of the rescue party come across a swamp where actor he rest of the rescue party come across a swamp where gonzales and two others leave the group. The rescue party makes their way across a giant fallen log, when t-rex attacks the rescue party. yieson, Choy and several other crewmen are killed after being thrown off the log by spino to the bottom of the cliff, and the rest of the crew is shaken off the log into a ravine; eugene's camera is destroyed as well.eugene returns to and rescues her from three *spinosaurus rex*, killing them. allosaurus scares the mighty giants away and creates a herd of brachiosaurus stempe.they run for their lives.

M-G soldiers fly with their chopper giving eugene and rico some aerial support. They keep on shooting the allosaurus.then the chopper gets ambushed by a pteranodon and crashes down to the ground.
M-G soldier 1 :Is everybody ok .is everyone alright.M-G soldier replies yeah I think so ,except i think i broke my leg.I can't feel my legs ,this thing got my feet . M-G soldier: keep calm men,we'll help you.

Wow where are we.M-G soldier 1: I am not sure.M-G soldier 2 :it's some types of relocation .M-G: soldier 2 :relocation for what.not sure

M-G soldier 1 : we should keep moving.As they keep moving they end up trapt in a gate.M-G soldier : wait, it's a trap.M-G soldier 1 : trap for what.M-G soldier: they are letting in something. Oh my god.Shoot it,shoot it.a pack of utahraptors on the loose.

Two of the M-G soldiers wounded and the rest fall back. M-G soldier 1 : fall back,fall back everyone.

Aside from situation of the M-G soldiers Eugene and rico make it to the control room where they need search and rescue.

This is rico comin .this is rico , I need search and rescue immediately the coordinates from earth is 30 kilometers west 30 degrees.10 degrees north and 20 degrees.3 part land 1 part water.Operator: and what is this planet called.Eugene: I think eurora.

The t-rex out of nowhere attacks base camp where rico and eugene is near the control room is located at. The t-rex runs a rampage causing havoc and chaos. The M-G soldiers use bazooka,fire hose,and dinosaurs net but, none of them worked.

Rico says i know what have to do.as he prepare for battle.he gears up with mech suit.then he says to the rex get away from their youu over grown gecko come and get your throat cut. T Rex roars and fights rico. Every dinosaurs gets loose like trench warfare.the dinos battle the colonial marines like a war in vietnam.it's a near suicide.it had to stop.although not many have survived. Rico sacrifices for the team by falling behind gear up to stop a tyrannosaur and utahraptor and gets eaten while others escapes.rico: come on you ugly piece of shit.come and get your throat cut.tyrannosaur and utahraptor yells and roars.ahhhhhhhhhhhhhhhhhh. Is that it is that best best you can do.come on.this is gonna sting a little.t-rex and utahraptor slices and dices while the bomb go off and rico rests in piece. Eugene did you get any fossils or anything that is useful,all i got are those dinosaur eggs.really where although,that is not accurate is it.Eugene : no.Alright then.
 Lieutenant Jericho come in lieutenant Jericho.god damn there is no communication .I have to go find another way to contact the helicarrier. Wait here jericho.I hope this would work we have to get off this planet. We should find a space shuttle and get off this planet.THere one shuttle in garage lab but it's nearly broken. We have to find a way to get this shuttle started.how in world christen aderson are we going to search and rescue the crew my crew half of em is deceased .

Well then i got nothing to say then jericho.where is that guy he was supposed to be back by now ,I hope nothing happened to him like he's dead .where is everyone.i sure knew he was here few minutes ago.oh my god the lizards completely torn lumpy apart

It's a no go we have to find another guy to communicate through search and go.how about you man.me i'm just a communiaction guy. Wifi intact it's a no go gentlemen.

As the t-rex approaches the helicarrier it lurk on human with it's narrow jaw and preys on them. T-rex is a scavenger says jericho says it will prey on not one but all of us.

As the spino attacks a rampage the velociraptor rex stumble on land with the crew of colonial marines

The raptor is pack hunter says jericho it will prey on everything and everyone.no man can stan up to the these beasts.Definetly avoid them.there an open passege in the jungle.damn .we have to across the marshy swamps.there no other way to avoid the raptors this is the only way.happy now jericho.we have to go inside the tunnel.yeah it's too dark.i got lighter jericho it should help.look over there .eugene i got a sniper rifle.i you want it just ask for it.jerico.look behind you!!the raptors are attacking .clear the passage.look behind you.oh my god!!!help!!! Jericho nooooo!!!!!

The team stumbles on heard of brachiosaurus.as they go by the boat.they struck on a sick dinosaur.they find a secret hidden passage.where the stream of heavy nile waterfall.they found a cave of pteranodons.as they enter the cave the pteranodons attack.oh my god.what is it says jericho.sir it's a bird cave. For what ? ah!!!help!!!lieutenant jericho. Come in jericho.we are surrounded by dinos.it's tearing us apart. Please help us.

Eugene and jericho fight of the raptors by using archer and heavy sniper.eugene and jericho all surrounded by raptors.oh my god says jericho. Eugene: with me jericho.after they got all the raptors squared away they go to the lab to retrieve some fire crackers and lots of smoke ammunition.as they go to lab they find a tank.hey what about this .yap this will definety work.

Choppers in rescue position team of scientists gets rescued and the other team falls behind.
Search and rescue.hey what about the others says eugene.there's no time we got to go.
Second helicarrier will rescue the marines.there not much space in the helicopter.i was thinking
the same how are we going to save those colonial marines there's not much space, in the
helicarrier.well i'll have to make two trips then i guess.

The team takes extra precaution and battles the monsters off.as they battle dinosaurs they also fire 19 bullets on the spinosaurus.they use heavy fire arms on the beasts.monsterous beasts are killed and slaughtered in the process.one team uses heavy gunfire while other use smoke granade.they clear the path of journey.

The team spots herds of ankylosaur,triceratops and gallimimus.they look out for another helicarrier and a space shuttle.where can they be rescued.they try to fix the broken chopper.

But none prevails.as jericho wonders where is the jet so he can smoke out the raptors.as he get 35 ammunition he fires.die you sucker die says jericho.

© Keiji Terakoshi

Pteranodon

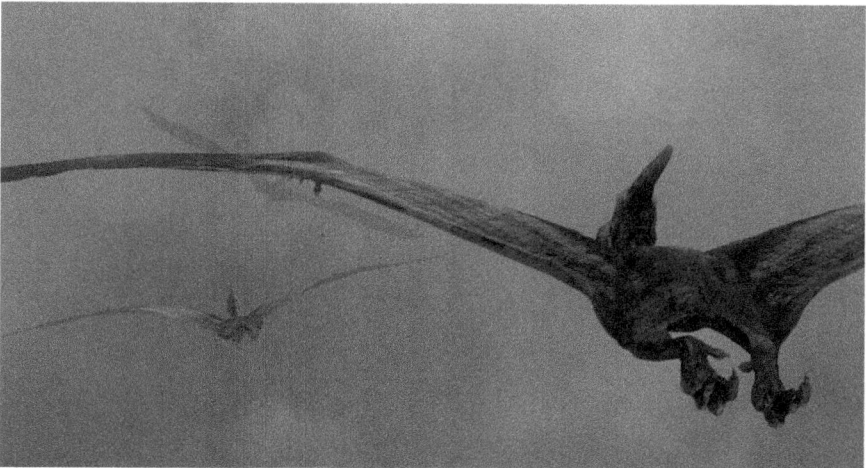

As rescue coppers arrive the team sees herd of pteranodon flying by in the air.then they go home to earth.they are home safe and sound as they walk by the door of whisky company they are each rewarded with 100 dollar check .

www.ingramcontent.com/pod-product-compliance
Lightning Source LLC
Chambersburg PA
CBHW072017280526
45788CB00005B/2083